SOCIAL MEDIA MARKETING
Use Social Media to Grow Your Business and Make More Money

Table of Contents

Introduction

More than 2 billion people own a Facebook account. Also, these people use Facebook at least every month. For that reason, Facebook has become the most popular social network in the whole world. The average Facebook user spends more than an hour every day on the network.

A lot has changed since Facebook was launched in the market. Today, there are so many things that Facebook can do that many of us thought would not be possible. For example, it can host a 360-degree video and sell products through a Chatbots among many others.

It's not just the number of people that use Facebook, but the amount of attention that Facebook gets from us. To most users, Facebook is like the Internet. They can't put down their phones. That aside, are you struggling to market your business using Facebook?

Pages are the best ways for businesses to market. A Facebook page is a public place that allows your fans to "like" the brand, business, celebrity, or even an organization. Fans can receive an update to content on the Page through their News Feed. On the other hand, the business can increase brand awareness, track advertising, gather insights, and communicate with users.

Inside this book, you'll find everything that you need to know to start social media marketing using Facebook. Regardless of whether your business has a Page or it is your first time, this book is for you. We shall start by defining Social Media Marketing before we dive deep into Facebook.

Chapter 1: Getting Started with Social Media Marketing

What is Social Media Marketing?

Social Media Marketing is a branch of internet marketing that involves the production of content and sharing it on a social media network. Social networks may include Facebook, Instagram, Twitter and many more. Social media marketing may involve simple tasks such as posting an image, text, updates, and video that captures the attention and involves the audience.

The social media sector is massive. It is one of the fastest growing fields in the history of the world. In fact, the rate of growth seems to be much quicker than the growth of the internet.

Basics of Social Media Marketing

When you try to familiarize yourself with the modern social media, the chances are that you'll be overwhelmed. There's so much in the social space that was not there a decade ago.

Traditionally, you could see a few business profiles. But today, it is a must to have a social presence for your business, with 80 percent of the marketers depending on social media to increase their brand awareness.

If you feel that you are late, no need to panic for this section will introduce you to the basics.

If you are going to start from scratch, we shall provide you with a list of social media basics that will help you discover your presence. Whether you have an interest in customer service, social selling or anything, this basic will help you to get started.

Select your social channels

First things first, you must select where your business is going to be?

A big brand that commands a large customer base should have a social presence across all the social media channels. Giant businesses such as Starbucks and McDonald's usually have resources that ensure they are everywhere. But what if you are a small business?

Since you will need to narrow down, you must select a channel that you are going to concentrate. Below is an overview of each of the leading social platforms.

Instead of trying to focus on all of them, you must choose the type of platforms that are realistic based on your target audience and industry.

Social network sites worldwide ranked by number of active users (in millions, as of January 2017,)

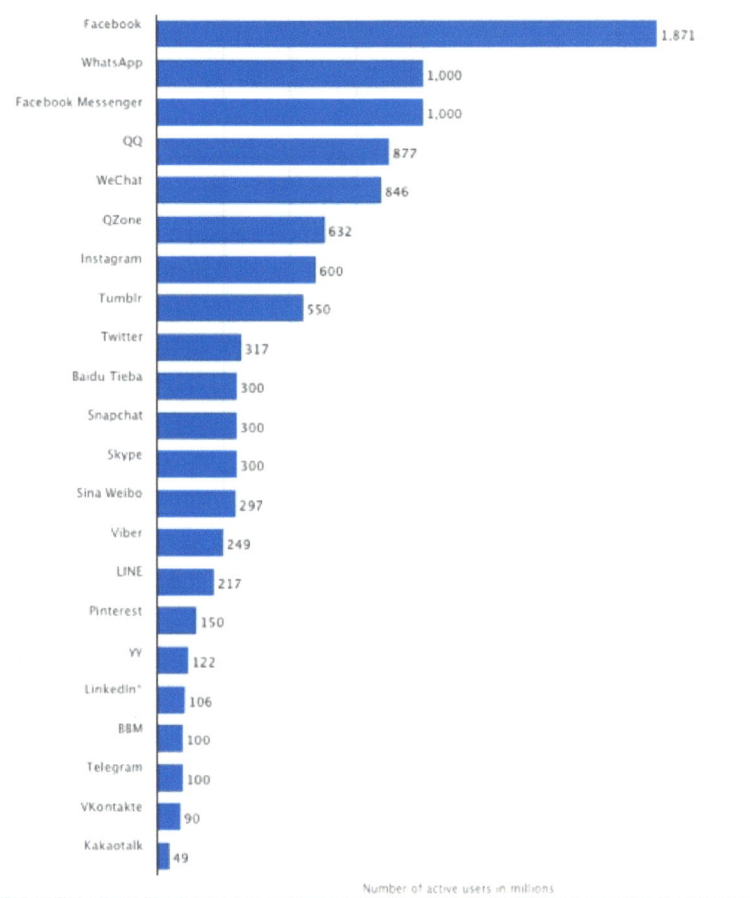

Number of active users in millions

Twitter

Twitter is a high starting point for any business. First, it requires the least setup and offers the best platform to engage with customers. There is a good reason why Twitter is considered as the go-to platform for customer service. If you want to master the basics of social media marketing using hashtags and the language of social media etiquette, then Twitter is the place to focus on.

Facebook

Facebook is the biggest name in social networks. Facebook platform is the best standard for social media ads if you are interested in a paid promotion. Similarly, it is essential to have a social profile of Facebook, especially for a brick-and-mortar business. It will give you the best platform to support check-ins and reviews. It is an excellent place to grow a local following.

Instagram

At the center, Instagram features a network that is focused on visual content. This is a significant platform for brick-and-mortar business, influencers, and e-commerce shops. This platform requires brands to get creative. It has eye-popping photos, clever captions, and unique means to identify what a person is selling.

LinkedIn

This is a network that is concerned with trends and networking. While most business profiles usually belong to a startup, LinkedIn is an excellent platform for an individual interested in a network in a B2B space. If you want to get in touch with an influencer, CEO, then chances are that you will find them here.

Pinterest

This is a visual platform that is highly popular with the millennials. This is also the best platform for social selling. Unlike Instagram, Pinterest is focused on imagery and motivational content where the products are at the forefront.

YouTube

While YouTube may not be considered as a traditional social network, this platform has an active community that is good for marketing. Since the video is the primary mark of identification, and the form of content across many platforms. YouTube is the best platform to upload videos if you are ready to create them.

If still you feel confused and you don't know where to start, you can ask yourself where most of your competitors and audience spend time?

Fill your social profile

One of the most important basics of social media marketing is to complete your social profile. For you to ensure that you can compete well in the market, you must ensure that your profile is 100 percent complete. Not only does this make your profile appear professional, but it also makes it easy for your business to be found.

Think about it this way, the results of social media tend to come first for any small business on Google.

This means that by filling your profile with your business details, and other relevant information, it is going to be easy for you to be found in a Google or native social search.

Although every network has its own details, there are specific things that you need to complete in your profile.

Business name and URLs
If your business has a unique name and a specific number of characters, then you don't have to think twice about the choice of your URL. However, it is not a must to use the same URL if you want to register with different platforms. Big brands such as Nike do this so that the fans don't get confused.

When trying to search for a name, you can decide to use NameChk to help you brainstorm and confirm that your choice is present.

Choose a brand creative and image
Your cover photo and profile pictures must identify your business. If you are using a brand creative that is already there, make sure that your photos have been optimized correctly. There is nothing worse than a photo that makes your business appear unprofessional.

In case you want to create from scratch social photos, you will have to look for tools such as Canva that has different types of pre-made image templates to use.

Complete "bios" and "about" sections
Using the best content, describe your business most interestingly. Sometimes, people choose to look at the social media results before they can visit your website. That is the reason why you need to make sure that your contact information is up-to-date.

Follow businesses, prospects, and famous brands
There is little that you will get from your social presence if you are a total island.

By following other people, it sends a message that you are active in the social space. Whether it is prospects, leaders in the industry or competitors, make sure that you follow active profile to get a look at the way they run their business.

Specific networks provide a person with follower suggestions to help him or her to get started. Following the social profiles of others, can help you get inspired as you continue to learn more about your social media marketing basics.

Maintaining a close eye on your mentions
Before you start to worry about your content followers, it is vital to ensure that you have a system in place to help you track your notifications and mentions. Be ready to respond to a customer alert, a shoutout from a fan or even a new

follower from a prospect. Time is essential when it comes to responding to the touchpoints, this primarily related to customer service.

When you are working on diverse platforms, you must have tools to help you with the monitoring. By integrating a direct response into your platform, it is going to be difficult for you to miss a chance to interact with your followers and fans regardless of their comment.

Setting up your content strategy

Now that you have set up your profiles, then you must be ready to choose what you want to post daily. This is the time when you need to have a content strategy plan. Although this may appear like an additional task, it really depends on your goals.

- Do you want to educate your audience in the B2B space? Publish opinions, news, and relevant content.
- Do you want to market your e-commerce products? Post photos of your products and shots of others displaying their swag.
- Concentrate on customer service. Shout-outs, tips, and business updates.

No matter what you want to post, creating a hashtag to go along with your content is a brilliant move to make. If you are using the Twitter platform, a hashtag can be the best approach to get attention and encourage people to share their photos and interact with your brand.

Gather your content calendar

If you want to save time, then you must plan in advance. By planning it means knowing what you want to post, and when you are going to post it. Having the right plan will prevent you from posting the same pieces of content again and again. By tapping in the optimal time for interactions, it is possible to automate the most difficult features of your social presence without any fear of posting in real time.

Interact with others

It is important to note that social media is not about you alone. Social media marketing is all about how you interact with your audience - from the comments made on the posts, content published and getting others noticed in the social media. Engaging with fans and customers provides you with the right ground to say about your personality and introduce your brand to new followers.

Make it a habit to interact with some of your profiles every day. By focusing on building an interpersonal relationship can earn you major points with your followers.

Discover the voice of your brand

When it comes to personality, the best strategy to improve your level of socialness is by defining the voice of your brand. The point is to ensure that you present yourself as a human instead of a robot. You should aim to get real with your audience and followers. One way of getting real with them is to ensure you crack jokes with your followers. Jokes tend to create an easy to interact relationship.

Market your social channels

Let's imagine that all your social profiles are set up.

Well, how would you like followers to find you? Don't fall into the trap of restricting your social presence to social media. Look for other places where you can hype up your profiles. Some of these places may include:

- Site headers and footers
- Email newsletters, signatures and footers.
- Cross-promotion between social sites.
- In person using business cards.

Track the growth of your social presence

To get the pieces of your social presence running is a great relief.

But your job is far from being done. To ensure that you remain in front, then you must monitor the growth of your business. This is the time when you must have special tools that can send you daily reports on the way your content is performing. These reports are vital because they will help you to realize areas that you need to change and improve.

So how should you get started?

Getting Started with Social Media Marketing

When you are ready to step in and run your social media marketing, remember the following steps:

Choose the type of goals that you want to optimize.

Are you interested in finding new employees or you want to set up a thought leadership? Create a discussion and build a relationship to nurture the leads. The goals that you decide will direct you to the next step.

Pick the platforms that will benefit your business well

Here, you must remember that you want to start small and maintain the followers on each site. Having this in mind, choose one or two platforms that would benefit you the most. Most businesses prefer Facebook. However, the second social network you select will depend on your business. If you are in the B2B sector and you want to create thought leadership, then LinkedIn is the best place to choose. On the other hand, if you have a product that would perform well in visual marketing, Instagram is the best place to go.

Come up with a content schedule
A content calendar would help to map the type of content you want to share, and when you have prepared it in advance, it means you will not miss any opportunities.

Look for streams of curated content
The content that you need to share is extensive. And so, you need to curate the content. It is advised to look for different competing influencers and businesses that have content that is appropriate to your audience. Then you can continuously plan to share the content on platforms such as Pinterest, Twitter, and Facebook.

Monitor everything carefully
This is the time when you need to sit back and learn the type of content that users are interacting with, and the social trends. Most importantly, pay close attention to your pages for any chance to interact with new followers. Respond to questions that users ask immediately. Send thank you cards and responses for user reviews, and engage with the comments as often as possible. This is the best way for you to create a relationship with your community.

Chapter 2: Elements of Social Media Marketing

Before we look at the elements of social media marketing. Let's review some of the benefits of social media marketing.

Most entrepreneurs believe that social media marketing is the game changer when it comes to launching a business. As a result, it is an important sector that must be taken advantage of while it is still on the rise. However, some entrepreneurs think that social media marketing has no practical advantage but merely hard to learn.

Aspects that Define Social Media Marketing

Regardless of what your thoughts are about social media marketing, it has earned a reputation by many businesses as an essential tool in marketing. In fact, a report by HubSpot indicated that 92 percent of marketers in 2014 considered social media marketing as crucial in their businesses. Besides, 80 percent of the responses reported an increase in traffic after integrating social media marketing. Below are some of the aspects that define Social Media Marketing.

It raises the awareness of your brand
Every chance that presents itself for you to publish content and boost your brand awareness is critical. Social media channels represent the voice of your brand. The social platforms make it easy for new customers to identify your business. For instance, a regular Facebook user may come across a newsfeed that defines

your business. Or, even a customer may discover your business by scanning through your profile.

It increases the loyalty of the brand

Based on a report released by Texas Tech University, brands that participate in social media channels have higher customer loyalty. The report recommended for companies to make use of the tools designed for social media function. When you have an open and strategic social media plan, it could be vital in increasing the brand loyalty of customers. In a separate study carried out by Convince & Convert, 53 percent of Americans who follow brands in social networks are very loyal customers.

Better rates of conversion

There is no argument on this. Social media marketing will result in better rates of conversion in different ways. The most important feature is the humanization element that happens because brands are humanized through social media interactions. Social media is a platform that brands can take advantage, and this is necessary because people enjoy doing business among themselves, and not with companies.

Other studies also realized that social media channels account for 100 percent leads than outbound marketing. Also, it contains the most significant number of followers. This often increases credibility, trust and represents social proof. For that reason, building an audience in social media can help boost the conversion rates.

Big opportunities to convert

Before you can publish a post on any social network, you must think of it as a means to market your business. When you create a page to post updates, treat it as an opportunity to get new followers. In other words, this page will give you the chance to interact with your followers. Don't waste that opportunity. Treat each post, video, image or comment you share as an avenue to interact with your customers. If you can spend time to respond to different comments posted by your followers, it will indicate that you are active and concerned. Such actions make a follower to consider you as a reliable person. The long-term effect is that it may lead to real conversion. However, not every interaction may necessarily result in a conversion, but if you aim to leave a positive feeling to every user you interact with, you will increase the probability of conversion.

Higher brand authority

When you regularly interact with your social media customers, it sends a positive message about your personality. When a customer is impressed by your service, the first place that they will want to go to send a compliment is in the social media network. If they post the name of your company or business name, this will automatically increase the chances of getting new followers and customers. When a lot of people are speaking good about your company or business, the more valuable your brand becomes. Don't forget that when you interact with social media influencers, it also boosts the brand visibility.

Inbound traffic increases

If social media is unavailable, inbound traffic will only be accessible to persons that know the brand and individuals that are searching for keywords to help them rank. Each social media profile that you add should act as a platform to convince people to come to see your site. Also, every content that is created for the company profile should be interesting to the reader. When you have exciting and quality content, it tends to increase your inbound traffic.

A better search engine ranking

SEO is one of the best ways that you can showcase relevant content from search engines, but the strategies keep changing. It is not enough to change your content daily on your blog, you still need to optimize the content, and distribute links that refer to your site. Search engines like Google calculate ranking by using the presence of social media. One of the reasons for this is that a strong brand must use social media. This means that it is important for one to have an active social media account so that it can signal to search engines that you have a credible and legitimate brand. In other words, if you would like to rank for a particular set of keywords, it is necessary to have a strong social media presence.

Better customer insights

Social media will also provide a chance to learn insights about customers and what they are interested in. For instance, you can track down the comments and analyze the way people consider your business. It is possible to personalize your content based on a given topic and understand the type of content that delivers interest. Still, you can take advantage of the various promotions published on different social media platforms and identify the perfect combination to create revenue.

A great customer experience

Every customer that you get an opportunity to interact with has to feel satisfied with your service. As such, you need to ensure that you are well prepared to answer any questions that they may have. If you can leave a customer feeling excited about your service, then you can be sure of gaining conversion rates. Besides just getting a conversion rate, excellent customer experience is going to build the best relationship with your followers. When a customer criticizes your product, the way you will respond is essential. Don't mess up but accept the criticisms and show that you noted the points highlighted. The best thing that you need to ensure is that you make the customer know that you care.

There are many benefits of making sure that you have a long-term social media campaign. However, if you still doubt whether to get your feet into social media marketing. Below are additional points to consider:

- **Your competitors are already using social media.** When your competitors are using social media tool, it means that the possible social media traffic that you could command is being taken over. Don't allow your competitors to take up all the benefits. In case your competition is not taking part in social media marketing, then you even have a good reason to get started.

- **The earlier you start, the better you get the benefits.** In the industry of social marketing, companies and small businesses try to establish a long-lasting relationship with their followers. In other words, if you can start early, then you are sure of building a long list of followers.

- **Possible losses are insignificant.** As a matter of fact, social media marketing will not cost your business in any way. So you don't need to fear that you are going to register a significant loss. For example, the costs of setting up a profile and creating marketing ads may not be more than $500. Don't wait or feel worried about losing your money. If you can follow the right steps and guidance, you will have a lot of customers, and increase traffic. Higher traffic has the probability of a higher conversion rate.

Elements of Social Media Marketing

Social media is a great tool to use to market. About 90 percent of adults have social network accounts. Also, they use the accounts as channels of communication with their brands.

As of today, social media has become the most important method of marketing. Whether you plan to start your business or you are just about to launch your first social media campaign, there is always something that you can earn to enhance your approaches.

Below are elements that you must consider to have the best social media campaigns.

Build an audience persona

The main point of effective social media marketing is to address a specific audience using social posts. This means that if you don't know who your audience is, you will need to take time to develop an audience persona.

An audience persona involves in-depth research that tends to defines more about your audience. This includes fears, interests, behaviors, and needs. An audience personal should include the persona's goals and pain points.

When you have a great idea about your audience, it will assist you in selecting social media platforms that they tend to use a lot

Setting goals and objectives

When you have an excellent idea of the character of your audience, you'll need to determine the main goals for your social media marketing efforts. What are you looking forward to achieving with your plan? The primary goals for most of the social media business marketing campaigns include:

- Building a brand awareness
- Lead generation
- Getting a website traffic

Whatever goals that a person decides to choose, it is essential for the goals to be in line with the different metrics that can be applied to measure success.

When there are no goals and metrics, it becomes difficult to determine ROI, and identify whether the efforts are effective.

Team building and resourcing

Research has indicated that creating an actual social media strategy is harder for small businesses and enterprise organizations. This is because social media businesses prefer outsourcing than build their teams. The most significant decision that you need make is whether your staff can take care of the social media marketing approaches or you will want to outsource. Remember, finding a person who can create your social campaign and communicate with your audience is not easy. Some social media marketing activities will be easy to complete with tools whereas others will be a bit complex. Below are tools that you can use to make it easy to create your social media campaigns:

- **Social media automation tools:** You can use Buffer or Hoot suite and schedule your social posts to go out at optimum times.

- **Social following tools:** This tool is used to manage FollowerWonk and ManageFlitter.

- **Blog aggregator tools:** Use a tool like Feedly to help you aggregate your blog feeds into a single place.

Research

Once you are aware of the person who is going to facilitate your campaigns, and the kind of tools that they will use to create it, the next thing to do is to dive into research.

- The posting strategy
- The campaign content

The social media campaign will likely include a combination of native content and sharing content with others.

For this reason, you may have to take time to search for relevant memes, blog post, and other social network content to share. Buzzsumo is a great tool that can help you achieve the functions. You also need to use this time to look for content types that generate the right response from your target audience.

Then you can start to research your posting approach. How often are you supposed to post, and on what kind of platforms? According to research done by HubSpot, it found out that the best time to post on Facebook includes:

- 3 PM on Wednesdays
- 12-1 PM on Saturdays
- 1-4PM on Thursdays and Fridays

The number of times that you can post your content will depend on the social network channel.

Selecting a platform

An average user of social media has five accounts. This means that if you want to reach out to your target audience in a practical way, you may need to look for them in other networks. However, that does not mean that you go open an account with every platform. The best way when starting a social media marketing campaign is to use 1-2 platforms. You need to examine yourself and see whether the available resources and time on your side can help you manage. But just make sure that you don't stretch yourself so much.

Again, you don't want a situation where you have a social profile that you last updated 8 months. That is why you need to choose your platform wisely. If you are confused about which platform to go with, think about how the platform is related to your business goals. Facebook is the best if you want to build your brand royalty, while LinkedIn is excellent for B2B business development.

Chapter 3: Know Your Audience

Now that you are well versed with the basics of social media marketing. Let's dive deep into Facebook marketing. The most significant advantage that Facebook advertising commands is the ability to identify and focus on a specific audience. Even though this is possible, many Facebook marketers continue to struggle to address the right group that they can convert. If you're one of them, read on to learn how you can link up with your specific audience and turn them into customers.

Based on reports released in the Q4 2017 earnings, Facebook ad revenue increased by 48 percent year-to-year. This means that marketers across the world are using Facebook advertising at a high rate. Also, this report reveals the massive opportunity that Facebook provides to marketers.

That aside, a massive ad spending doesn't mean that your business is going to generate more revenue. If your ads, don't reach to the right audience, no matter how good they may appear, your business will not fulfill its goals. In other words, you will be just wasting your money on ads.

To avoid wasting your budget and generate revenue from your Facebook ad, you must optimize your conversions, and for you to maximize your conversions, you must learn how to target the right audience. Below we show you how you can do it.

First, you must learn about your potential audience. Getting to learn more about your audience is the most important thing that will help you to reach out to them. The reason is that the more you know your followers, the more you'll try to create customized content and the higher the probability that your ads will achieve its objectives.

Remember that getting in touch with your audience doesn't just involve sending out content to a specific number of users. To realize your Facebook marketing goals, you must ensure that you catch the attention of your followers. Then you can get them to convert.

And to realize that, you need to create audience personas.

Learn About Your Audience Personas

Traditionally, marketers used to reach to their audience based on location and demographics. Although these elements are a high starting point, they are not likely to deliver the best results.

Today, marketers are advised to administer cross-channel audience analysis based on interests and behaviors to help them learn more about the audience personas.

When you understand your audience, you will know the content format and topics that they are likely to enjoy and drive them towards conversion.

When you publish ads that don't resonate with your audience, you register a loss. For example, Facebook ads that aren't customized to the correct audience record a low score of relevance and are quite expensive.

The modern consumers aren't interested in irrelevant ads; this is explained by the rising number of ad blockers. Also, modern consumers want a personalized experience. For instance, more than 30 percent of users prefer individualized ads.

The significance of searching for audience personas has continued to be ignored by many marketers. For example, 27 percent of marketers don't carry out customer research. This means that if you can take some time to study and analyze your audience, you will have the upper hand when advertising using Facebook.

Therefore, the secret to Facebook advertising is first to analyze your audience to learn about their interests and behavior. Once you have done the analysis, you can move on to create personalized content. Another thing that you should be keen to look at when reviewing the personas include:

- Find out their medical social activity.
- The kind of influencers they follow.
- The stage of the customer journey that they are in.
- Page affinities.

In case you are wondering how you can access all this kind of information; the answer is to look for data. Keep in mind that your audience is available on different online platforms. So the process of looking for your personas should depend on cross-channel data that extends from social networks to websites.

Well, how can you get in touch with your Facebook target audience?

Reaching to Your Target Audience on Facebook

Once you have found out whom to get in touch on Facebook, the next thing that may start to bother you is how to deliver your content to the right audience. There are different ways that you can go about with the following case. The methods work both for ads and content.

If you plan to use Facebook ads, then you can apply Facebook's advanced targeting options to reach out to your audience. This will assist you in grouping your followers so that you can only deliver your content to users that are likely to convert.

Below are some of the options that you can apply to group your audience:

Location
At least there is one region where you want to show your Facebook ads. The geo-tagging function will assist you in choosing users based on the region, city, country, which is good to help you narrow down your audience.

Demographics
Usually, products and services are designed to fulfill the needs of a particular user. The demographics ad based targeting is effective at targeting users who share common characteristics with your customers. This also increases the probability of conversion.

Behaviors and interests
These features are critical in modern marketing because 71 percent of consumers like personalized ads. Furthermore, ads customize to users record a higher click rate than that not personalize to users. That is the reason why behaviors and interests are critical.

Breakdown of Interests and Behavior Types to Use for Targeting

Interests
Family, food and drink, sports and outdoors, hobbies and activities, fitness and wellness, business and industry, entertainment.

Behaviors
Digital activities, media, automotive, seasonal and events, expats, charitable donations, mobile device user, media, travel, residential profiles.

Custom Audiences
You can take advantage of Facebook custom audiences to retarget users based on Facebook ID, phone number, website, app, email, and content activity.

Lookalike Audiences

This kind of audience is designed by Facebook depending on the characteristics of the current audience. Creating a lookalike audience that convert can be more comfortable when you have data that is defined based on personas and audience.

When you do the right targeting, it tends to increase your Facebook relevance score. This score is important because when it is low, it will decrease the advertising cost. As such, it is advised to take time and understand your audience before running Facebook ads. To achieve that, you must be ready to conduct an audience analysis and redefine your targeting methods. In the long run, it will save you money.

Reaching to an Audience Through Excellent Content

You'll do more on Facebook than just running a targeted ad campaign. Aside from Facebook ads, reaching to your right audience highly depends on the relevance of your content and the ability to start valuable conversations.

That is the reason why you need to prioritize your audience analysis so that you can have great content. By knowing your followers, it will give you the chance to select topics that they are interested, participate in a conversation, and command authority on the subject. As a result, your content will be great in generating the best results.

Besides creating quality content, other ways that you can use to reach your audience on Facebook include:

Facebook groups

This is where you create a group for your Facebook page. This will provide you with the opportunity to build an interactive community within your business.

Influencers

If you know some of the influencers that may rhyme with your audience, then that is the best chance to work with them and take advantage of their platform to get in touch with the correct user group.

Facebook events

Set up an event that is connected with the interest of your audience. This particular event should help you to group users that you want to embrace in one central place.

So far you know how to get in touch with your Facebook audience, but how can you get them to convert?

Driving Your Target Audience to Conversion

Growing your audience until it reaches that stage of conversion using Facebook ads and other types of content, should always be determined by the stage in which your followers are at.

The purchase internet isn't the same for every user. A person that comes across your Facebook page today is at a different conversion stage than a person who has interacted with your content and visited your online eCommerce store.

In other words, some users will need to read a lot of content before they can purchase your product. Some will be ready to buy once the ad attractively appeals to them.

That is the reason why you need to pay attention to the buyer's journey when you create Facebook content.

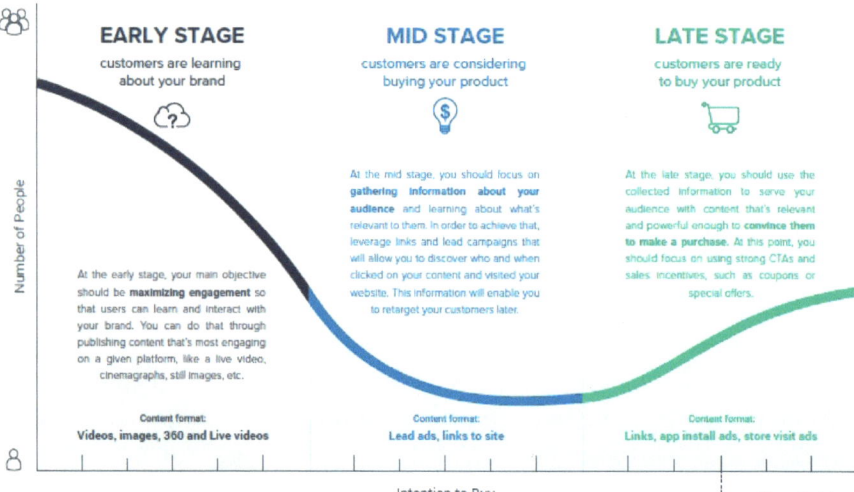

A quality ad is essential to convince your target audience towards conversion. So make sure that you use high-resolution, compelling visuals that rhyme with the specifications of the platform.

Another technique that you can apply to drive conversions is to retarget. In this case, you can insert a snippet of HTML code that will monitor whoever visited your site.

If you use Facebook Pixel, then you can easily segment your Facebook audiences into those who interacted with a specific topic or campaigns.

It is also a great thing to use Facebook conversion ad objectives. They have conversions like app downloads, visitors to your website, and visiting your brick-and-mortar stores.

These ads will make it possible for you to optimize your conversion volume. The only thing that you need to pay attention is that you launch them at the right stage according to your followers' journey.

How to create Facebook Audiences?

To create and control your Facebook audiences, you must learn to use the Audience Manager Tool. This tool is found in the Business Manager. First, you will need to click on the top-right menu and choose "Audiences."

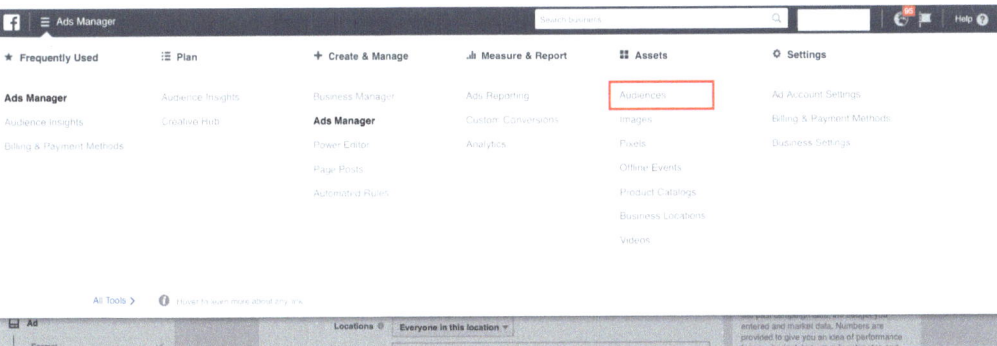

While on the Audiences page, here you can look at all your saved Facebook audiences and also create new ones. To ensure that you understand the wide variety of targeting options that Facebook provides. We shall start with the basics:

There are three major audiences on Facebook.

- Saved Audiences
- Custom Audiences
- Lookalike Audiences

Every type of audience has lots of options to help a person create the perfect target audience for the Facebook campaign.

Facebook Saved Audiences

This is the kind of audience that you can define by picking people's interests. For this type of audience, you can create it both on the campaign set up or in the Audience Manager.

Location-based targeting

This one you will be targeting people in specific places such as country, state, city, postal code and many more. Location targeting also exists in which you can even become more specific:

- Everyone found in this location
- People who live in this location
- People recently in this location
- People traveling in this location

Facebook Custom Audiences

This is perhaps the most high-value type of targeting because it gives you the ability to retarget past website visitors and people that have interacted with your app or content. There are different ways that you can set up a Custom Audience. Don't worry, we are going to look at each method briefly.

Custom Audiences from Customer Files

This deals with the existing customer files. This is a great way to target newsletter subscribers or even app users.

Custom Audiences from Website Traffic

Traffic from the website Facebook audiences can help you come up with remarketing techniques for people that have visited and interacted with your website. These represent a quality audience because the users that see your ads have already revealed an interest in it. To successfully create audiences based on website traffic you must ensure that you install Facebook Pixel.

In case your website is powered by WordPress, it is also possible to set up this type of Custom Audiences using a Pixel Caffeine plugin.

Once you have the Facebook Pixel installed, you can move to the Audience Manager and set up a Custom Audience based on past website traffic. This has different options to choose from. If you like, you may set to:

- Target specific people that visited certain pages.
- Target everyone who visited your page.
- Target people that haven't visited the website for a given amount of time.

Chapter 4: How to Market Facebook Pages?

Back then when businesses started using Facebook to market their products, Facebook pages were very simple. You could only like a business to follow them.

Businesses used to post visible content on their walls, and it was accompanied by a link to their website. That was during that time. Everything was kept simple.

Today, things have rapidly changed. Just like Facebook has changed its platform and added more features, businesses have not been left behind. Most businesses have embraced this change and redefined the way they market their products and companies.

In 2016, over 65 million businesses created Facebook pages. If you think that your niche is already tricky, Facebook can make that even more complicated. When you decide to market your business on Facebook, not only are you competing with your direct competitors but also for attention to everyone.

And that is the reason why you need to get everything right when creating your Facebook business pages. Unfortunately, most businesses still lag behind because they don't have the right Facebook business page that can generate attention and capture the interest of Facebook users.

The good thing is that by learning how to create a perfect Facebook business page, you will also learn how to become a great Facebook Business Manager. Facebook Business Manager is like behind the scenes of Facebook that gives you the ability to control and see everything on how your Facebook page is running.

As the admin of a Facebook Business page, you will always see a link at the top of the page designed for Facebook Business Manager.

When you access your page using the Facebook Business Manager, you get the same view of the page like users, but with some additional features. For example, you can perform any edits that you want on the page. Accessing the Facebook page as the Manager gives you a lot of features.

Your Facebook page will contain the following sections.

- Products
- Store
- Settings
- Business Info
- About
- Company Info
- Page Roles
- Cover Video
- Contact Info

Now, we are going to look at the most important sections that you must know for you to create a perfect Facebook business page.

Business Info

It might look simple, but that is not the case. In fact, it is very tricky. First, very little information appears in front of the Facebook business page. This means that for people to see your business info, they will need to click the "See All" button. Another way is to click the "info" button located at the side of the menu.

Since Facebook is an example of a content platform, the latest information will always come first before previous information. Even with that, the previous information is still essential, especially for new customers. The first thing that they will want to know is who you are? The Business Info part describes the mission of your business. Don't confuse it with what your company does? This section will come later.

When crafting a response for your Business Info, use this chance to shine, display your passion, and sell the mission of your business to capture the attention of people.

The About

The Facebook business pages have different sections that tend to overlap that you may get confused on what to write. For example, the About section and the Company overview are the same. As a result, most businesses fill these sections with the same information.

When about to write an about description for your business, keep in mind that the best "About description" is one that has one-sentence, and jumps straight to the point. A great example is CNN:

MORE INFO

ⓘ About
Instant breaking news alerts and the most talked about stories.

A different approach that you can use if you don't want to write a description is to add a quote. However, this should depend on the type of business you run. Think of a quote that will spark some flair.

Why the about section is significant, and you need to treat it with utmost seriousness is because anytime your business is tagged and Facebook users hover their mouse around the name, a box will pop up to show the information. So you should use this to drive people into your business.

Company Overview

While the about section and company overview may look similar, you should avoid writing the same thing on both sections. It is advised to write a functional description of your business or company in this section. You should craft something that is related to the value pitch of your business.

This section may appear boring to readers depending on the kind of business you run. However, you need to use this chance to reassure your future and present clients that you are serious. That is why you need to avoid any humor unless you just can't live without it.

Again, make sure that you use clear sentences that don't combine so many ideas. Even when you know that your business industry is specific, try and divide a description into short sentences.

The general rule that you should not forget is to keep this section short. There is a good reason why Facebook created the Story section. A one or two paragraph should be okay.

The Story Section

As the name suggests, this section requires you to narrate the journey of your business or company. The story should explain who you are and how did your business start?

- What are the values of your business and how do you adhere to them?
- Who are your founders? Are they unique?
- Where are you headed to as a business?
- Are there any unique features or events that make your business memorable?

Think of the story section as what a grandmother would say when about to narrate a story from the old times. You can think of a witty saying that sympathetically defines your business.

When a person decides to visit your Facebook business page to read your story, they actually want to learn more about you, so you should make them marvel once they have finished reading. Don't disappoint them.

Milestones

While creating your Facebook page, it is easy to be tempted to include the significant achievements of your business in your story.
If you feel you need to break up the events and explain the details, then the milestone section is the best place to do that. However, if you are not sure whether you need to fill this section, just to clear up any confusion, it not a must.

For many businesses that are just getting started, you may not have any milestones achieved.

In case you are searching for different versions of milestones, which are unique to your business, they can be in any of this category:

- When you released a new product
- When you participated in the funding
- When you achieved a specific number of customers.
- When you found a moment of recognition

In short, if it's something that you like to share out with your friends and people when you meet, then you can add it here.

Contact Info

If your business doesn't have contact info details, then you need to be serious. Remember, it is from the contact info that you begin to experience ROI from Facebook.
- Are people looking for you after coming across your page?
- Or they are your customers using Facebook to ask you questions?

Since Facebook has more than 2 billion people, it is right to conclude that the figure includes your customers too.

- Whenever there is a complaint, they will look for you on Facebook.
- When they want to send a compliment, they will come to Facebook.
- When they want to know you, they will check first on Facebook.

For that reason, you need to have flawless contact information.

If you have a local business, make sure that you include your address, telephone number, and other relevant information for people to know that you can be found in real life.

You need to put the following information over a map so that people can exactly find you if they look for you.

Another thing is that you must have a link to your website. Organic traffic that originates from Facebook is significant. Social networks have become an essential tool in searching. That is why you need to be found, and your page has to drive people near to you.

For your website, it should not feature content from your competitors. Additionally, it should not have notifications that are going to affect users.

But it should be the best place to convert users into customers. Direct your users there and avoid a lot of clicks between the visit to your Facebook business page and the buy button.

The contact part gives you the freedom even to include a Facebook Messenger handle plus a button for them to send you a message immediately.

The Store

Facebook has influenced the growth of e-commerce by including a blue button to its Business pages.

The store has a button called "Shop Now." When users click this button, they are redirected to the e-store link. This is the first sign to show that users can buy your products online. However, Facebook has even gone further to add a Shop feature. This feature allows businesses to list their products, and make it easy for visitors to shop directly. When a person clicks on a product, you see a product window with comprehensive information.

For one to buy, they will need to click the "Check out" button, at this point they will be re-directed to the e-commerce platform to complete the transaction.

Products

This is an excellent feature because it makes it possible for people to see and browse products without leaving Facebook. The first thing is to ensure that all your products have been uploaded to Facebook. Next, set the featured products. Featured products refer to the type of products that everyone can see when they visit your page. Facebook has stretched the limits of e-commerce, that means if e-commerce is one of your sales strategies, you must create product pages on Facebook.

Locations

Although many businesses are online, some businesses cannot be found online. In the following case, you need to ensure that you update all the information about your locations, contact information and the time of operation.

Settings

The setting features have a lot of things. However, there are different settings that you need to make sure are on. The first is page visibility. This determines whether your page is visible on Facebook. The moment the changes are modified; you should ensure that they appear visible.

Next, Visitor posts: Do you want to receive posts on your page in a manner that it will be visible to others?

In general, the best approach to apply is to ensure the sharing is on but with some moderation. This means that people can create a post and send it to you first before they publish it.

In most cases, people say good things that you would love to share, but still, some people may disagree with what you do.

Rather than giving people instant access to your fans, you need to prevent that information from coming out.

Next, if you believe that your business has an international focus, there are several things that you need to activate.

Country restrictions
You need to confirm that potential customers from different countries can see you. If you want just to show a page to viewers from a specific country, you can still do that using the setting.

Post in multiple languages
This will allow you to post in different languages rather than resorting to a single language. Creating different types of content for various regions is important.

Translate automatically
This feature will automatically change content when it is seen by people from different regions.

Cover Video

Facebook has been at the forefront of embracing change. Over the past few years, Facebook has introduced changes to its features.

The video is a unique way to ensure that your message reaches the right audience. In fact, users prefer to watch a video about a product instead of reading the information about the product.

Facebook is not just a platform for someone to post videos. It has gone ahead to include videos into its various functionalities. Today, you can place a profile as videos. This makes it possible for you to create an excellent experience for people who visit your page.

Page Roles

Doing everything on your own is difficult. You need to work with other people. As a result, Facebook makes it possible for you to realize this goal. Assigning different users with various responsibilities is possible.

Facebook Business Page Marketing Tips

Whether you are creating a brand new Facebook Page for your business, or you are just interested in optimizing your current page, you are in the right destination. Facebook has more than 2 billion active users. This means if you plan yourself well, you can make good money from your business.

But taking a photo, creating a few posts, and expecting it generate leads may not really work. There is no short cut to having an appealing Facebook business page. You just need to create a comprehensive page.

Now that you know how to create a perfect Facebook Business Page, these tips should help you optimize and fine tune it.

Avoid creating a personal profile for your business

Some Facebook marketers choose to create a personal profile for their brand instead of creating a Facebook page. If you do so, you tend to put yourself in a big hole that you can't come out quickly. Why? You will not manage to access other essential resources and functionalities that a Facebook page comes with. Additionally, a personal profile will mean that people have to send you a friend request when they want to interact with you, and that is something that you don't want to happen. Again, once you have set up your Facebook Business Page, don't create a "professional" profile that is linked to your business.

Put a recognized profile picture

It is important that you have a recognized profile picture. Keep in mind that this picture should send a message to your audience about your business. So you can set up a company logo for a large brand or something that really demonstrates your business. When you have a picture that the audience can recognize, it is easy to receive likes and be found by Facebook Search. When selecting a photo remember that Facebook keeps changing the picture dimensions.

Select an engaging cover photo

Next, you have to select an attractive cover photo. Because your cover photo will occupy the most space on your Facebook page, it is good to choose one that is of high-quality and engages with the mind of visitors. Don't forget that, the same way profile images change, the Facebook cover photo dimension constantly changes, so it is good to check every time on the official Facebook guideline page.

Avoid publishing mishaps with the Page roles function.

We know stories where folks posted content that was not supposed to be published on a social media page. Make sure that you assign Facebook Business Page roles only to those employees that require it because of the work that they do. Some training may also eliminate the confusion of whether they should press "publish" or schedule first.

Use a call-to-action button

Since this feature was introduced by Facebook, brands have taken advantage of it to market their respective businesses. Things like "Watch Video," "Book Now" and "Sign Up" can be customized with some content or even a URL.

Complete the about section with basic information, and add company milestones

While visitors cannot see the "About" text when they visit the Facebook Business Page, when they click or hover on the "About" option, the content pops up. The purpose of optimizing your about section so that it reflects your brand. By doing so, your audience will see sense on what your page means even before they take a look at it.

Make sure you post videos and photos to your timeline

Visual content has increasingly become a necessity of online presence. But that is because it is easy for it to be shared on social networks than any other type of content.

Although photos capture the moments and look of your brand, you need to spend a good amount of time and effort on video. About 24 percent of marketers rank video as a top priority from a report by the State of Inbound.

"Watch Video" is a call-to-action that Facebook has allowed brands and businesses to implement on their pages. For sure, it has increasingly become a popular means to consume content. But pre-recording videos is not the only means, research shows that people spend more time on a live video than a pre-recorded video. So you should not hesitate to treat your viewers with an in-the-moment scene of your organization, but always make sure that you are prepared before going live.

Identify the definite timing and frequency of your posts

One of the most important things that you need to consider for your Facebook content strategy is the frequency of your post, and when. If you are not going to post regularly, your viewers may not consider you as reliable or authentic. So you need to post always, but people can get annoyed of their newsfeed populated with your content.

This is the time when a social media calendar can be very useful. Just like other online content, it will help you to know when you are supposed to share a specific post. You will also need to alter your calendar different times, especially in the early moments when setting up your page.

Pin important posts at the top of the page

On Facebook, every time new content is posted, the old content is pushed behind. Sometimes, you want to feature a specific type of content even if you publish new posts. In the following case, you will need to "pin" the content on the page so that it can continue to feature.

Chapter 5: Putting It into Practice

There is no slowing down with Facebook. The number of Facebook users continue to increase every day. If you have a business, then you cannot avoid or ignore the power of Facebook marketing. But you just need to make sure that you have a unique marketing strategy. There are many potential customers to target on Facebook. However, with a large number of users on the platform, it takes time to narrow down and find your niche.

That is why we provide you with a Facebook Marketing Strategy that you can use to get started.

Define Facebook Goals

For every marketing strategy, it is a must to set goals for your specific niche. The reason why you need to have goals is to help you focus on the largest marketing needs.

If you are using Facebook for marketing, or you want to change a bit your current strategy, it is clear that there are needs you want to fulfill. While coming up with goals, make sure that you don't set up unrealistic goals that you will not achieve. Let your goals address your major problem. One way that you can create the best goals is by using Facebook tracking tools.

Below are examples of goals that you can set

- **Boost the quality of sales: To** improve the quality of your sales requires that you target the right customers. So by using a well-organized Facebook marketing plan, you can reach to your target audience. Keep in mind that a large pond doesn't mean you will get a bigger fish. You need to start by working on something that you know well to use Facebook as a means to increase your audience.

- **An effective means of recruiting.** Getting more followers on your page is not easy. But with the right plan, you can increase your followers.

- **A better edge on the industry.** If you feel like competitors are a step further from you, using social media monitoring tools, you can monitor, listen and get a report of all the social conversations that revolve around you.

While these goals may not focus on every challenge that business experience, but it demonstrates how you can set your goals.

Understand Your Facebook Demographics

Demographics play a major role in any marketing strategy. When we look at Facebook, it has more than 2 billion users who scroll their newsfeed daily, so it is important to understand the kind people you want to address.

Besides, you must know the current demographics because the network audience of Facebook changes with time.

Pick a Data and Schedule Your Facebook Content

Each social network has its own content format, but Facebook provides users with different methods. There is Facebook Live, Facebook stories, video and image posts. In other words, your business content strategy has many opportunities.

For your brand, you should focus on the quality of the content and what you think your audience expects to see from your page. But avoid creating a lot of promotions. It will annoy the users. The content that you create should be attractive, entertaining and useful to your audience. Highlight the value of your brand, and choose your audience.

Categories of Facebook Content (and how you can use it)

By now you should be aware of the significance of your content, but which specific type of content will work well for your brand? Below is a discussion of the different types of organic content for Facebook and how well you best use each one.

Status

The simplest type of content. It is a powerful way to communicate. This content type has new features such as large text, and an option to insert your text on a background that is colored. This feature can help you pass across your message to your followers in the most effective way.

Videos

The need for video has kept increasing in the recent past. Studies report that 43 percent of users would like to see a lot from marketers. But only 15 percent of videos are seen with sound. Ensure that your video is accessible, easy for someone to understand and always has captions. Keep in mind to create videos that will grab the attention of users.

Images
A post that is accompanied with images tends to be more interactive than posts without images. In other words, being visual pays. However, don't start to depend on images to do all the job. Try and put your effort on quality images. If users think your product is boring, then it is a high time to change and apply beautiful images to demonstrate the creative side of your brand. Motivate your users with virtual reality features.

Links
Links are the best when you want to share a video, news, and posts. Look for your most interactive content and share it with your users on Facebook. It is not easy to do organic marketing, but you shouldn't stop you from publishing content.

Facebook stories
These are short clips. The idea started with Instagram stories, which was from Snapchat Stories.

Facebook live
Live content will generate more engagement on Facebook. While the Facebook Stories continue to expand, you can wow your audience with a different flair of Go Live.

Schedule Facebook Content on your social media calendar
You don't want to post anything on Facebook just because you wanted to publish it. By planning content, it means that you focus time and effort on the quality of the post. This will provide you with the best chance to engage and motivate your audience.

Unfortunately, you will not always get the time to create content. That is the reason why we have different social media publishing tools that can assist you in staying on track.

Identify Your Facebook Ad Strategy

It is important that you put your effort on your social media strategy than what you are going to get. Remember that it takes time and patience to grow your brand and audience. This is something that you will need to learn.

Well, but there is one way that you can use to reach there, and that is social media advertising. Most importantly on Facebook. So far, there are about 4 million advertisers with a click-through rate of 0.9 percent. To advertise on Facebook is simple, but not easy. You will need to create your brand and demonstrate it using ads.

Focus on a higher brand awareness

When creating your Facebook ad campaign, make sure that they are cost-effective and relevant.

For those starting out, you will want to remain with the weekly or monthly spend to minimize useless clicks and too much exposure. Your ad spends can rise up fast when you don't target the right audience. This takes us to the next important point of relevancy.

It is important to ensure that your Facebook ad is relevant. Targeting a large audience is not bad. At the start, you want to identify what may work and what may not work. But relevance is an important factor in Facebook ads.

If you already have a custom audience, this should be the right moment to send them with content that suits their needs. Just ensure that the content offers something new and is to be recognized.

Choose on creative content

We shall not stop mentioning it, but the quality is more important than quantity. If you want to keep your followers and get more users, then you must learn to create quality content. Quality content is one that addresses the challenges that your users go through, and it tends to provide a solution to the problems that they experience. Some great features that your ad content should have are:

- **Identity:** Does it have any relation with your brand and displays your service or product? Are the logos and business colors well displayed?

- **Reward:** What benefits are viewers going to get? Are they going to receive a promo code, deal, or whitepaper?

- **Tone:** Is there uniformity in the tone of your content or it is just business?

- **Action:** It is a must for your content to trigger an action, which addresses the goals you set. A clear and precise call to action is fine.

Update the Facebook ad content

The Facebook ad content will appear in your users' newsfeed. In other words, your followers will see the content show up on their newsfeed often. But you don't want to annoy your followers with the same content every day because it will chase them away. To maintain your followers, you need to change the content of your Facebook ad. One of the worst things is when your content becomes stale with viewers. Make an effort to change your content after 1-2 weeks. Don't allow old content to damage your remarketing efforts.

You also need to create a spreadsheet and populate it with the main metrics. Each metric will display important insights, and allow you to see what you need to achieve with your ad:

- **Impressions:** If you experience problems with visibility, you will need to revisit your content and identify what can generate more impressions.

- **Click-through rate**. When traffic is important, monitor your CTR and identify areas that you need to change.

- **The cost to acquire.** If your objective is to reduce the budget, then you must monitor the cost and set either weekly or monthly goals.

Be the First to Engage with Your Audience

The main reason why social media networks were created was to ease communication. Therefore, these are platforms for conversation, sharing content and discussion. As a business, you should never forget the main reason why social media networks were created. In other words, conversation and interaction should be among the top priority.

You must try and be an example to your audience. Facebook is a great platform to take part in discussions or even chats about your industry. No restriction on the type of audience, your interaction can be with your audience or a different one. Leading by an example involves starting a discussion on your page, then let it flow. Respond to your followers and viewers.

Twitter is well-known for being a wonderful social customer care network, but don't make twitter cause you to forget Facebook. You can create a Facebook engagement by asking people questions that you know they will respond. And this is where understanding your industry or niche comes into play. But if you sit back and wait for your followers to engage, you will wait forever. While it is hard to reach to everyone, there are different ways that you apply to boost your engagement.

For instance, Zippo is a great tool to use to engage with users through comments and continues a discussion you left on Facebook.

Allow Your Whole Workforce to Use Facebook

The social network is one of the best places for an employee to communicate and raise complaints. However, when employees have shareable content, you can be sure that you will reach to their audiences. This improves your business when you get your content shared across the newsfeed of your employees.

But one of the biggest challenges that most businesses experience is the correct content to share. Employees can be grouped into two categories.

- Those who fear to share the content of the company or business on their Facebook.
- Those who are ready to share the content on their Facebook newsfeed.

According to a market report published by Bamboo, 54 percent of users don't know how to share the correct content and act as an advocate on social networks. This means that you have to spend the time to build advocacy to support these employees.

Provide employees with an opportunity to share

It begins with employee advocacy plan that will allow employees in a company to make use of their social media accounts such as Facebook.

Monitor and Analyze Facebook Marketing Strategy

A successful Facebook marketing plan requires in-depth analysis. If you already have a plan and would just like to improve it, then you need to make use of the Facebook analytic tool. Also, you should apply the competitor analysis feature.

To succeed, you must have insights on what works and what doesn't work. These seven steps should help you improve your Facebook marketing and determine the strategy that works best for your case.

Chapter 6: Top Three Tips with Facebook Marketing

Regardless of the industry that you focus on, Facebook marketing is not optional. You can't just ignore the benefits that Facebook marketing brings to a business. Avoiding Facebook can be similar to neglecting not having a website back in the 2000s.

To make the most of Facebook marketing, we created for the key tips that will help you to succeed.

Know Your Audience

You should learn how to talk to people by knowing who they are. Your Facebook marketing strategy will work if you know things that your audience enjoys. Fortunately, Facebook gives all the resources that you need to learn to understand your audience.

Converse with them (and Not at Them)

The reason why you are using Facebook is to build and market your brand. However, that does not mean that you can choose to talk about your services or products all the time. If you do so, then you are going to lose all your audience. But what you need to do is to encourage them to interact. The best Facebook pages focus on encouragement. In other words, they have a lot of likes, comments, and shares. That means if you would like your Facebook page to be successful, then you need to emulate what the best pages do.

Anytime you share your latest blog, take time to ask them to tell you what they think about it. Or you can ask questions that you know will grab their attention. Other means that you can apply to increase engagement include:

- Creating contests
- Quizzes and polls
- "Fill in the blank" posts
- "Caption this image" posts

Another method is by demonstrating a little of your personality. Obviously, you want to remain professional and showcase your business in the best way possible, but Facebook is a platform where people go to interact and relax. They will not respond to a post if they are feeling stressed.

So you can share images and videos of your team and some happy customers. Doing this proves to them that you are a real business but not a business that depends on robots.

When a client sends you a question or asks for help, be quick to get back to them. Above all, make sure that you keep things normal.

Keep it on Brand

You already know why it is important to personalize your content to suit the challenges of your audience. For your Facebook page to succeed, you must speak to your Facebook followers.

However, if your first goal is to attract customers, you will want to use Facebook to get the best leads, and later sell. But for some brands, not every user is a buyer. In fact, a big percent of your Facebook users aren't going to purchase your product. Sorry to say so.

But how can stay relevant and attract the right buyers?

The secret is to keep your content relevant to your brand. It is the content that you create that determines whether you will attract buyers or not. If you write the best content that offers a solution to buyers, then you can be sure to convert leads.

Conclusion

At this point, you should be able to set up a Facebook Page. You should be able to slowly get new followers, get new Likes, and look at discussions growing between you and your users. Even if your page has a dozen users, you should be able to grab their attention and make them love your posts. Keep in mind that your Facebook community grows slowly.

Now that you have learned everything that this book has to offer, there are a few things that you can do to ensure that your Facebook strategies keep improving. First, *you need to engage with your Facebook users*. Next, *know your audience*. If you can know your audience, then you can create personalized content for them.

Also, you need to make sure that you *create high-quality content that is easy to read and addresses the needs of your audience*. Lastly, *concentrate on conversations with your audience and not just traffic*.

Description

This should be between 300 and 500 words

- 100 of these words
- Should be used as bullet points
- Hyping up the most exciting
- Parts of the book

www.ingramcontent.com/pod-product-compliance
Lightning Source LLC
Chambersburg PA
CBHW041114180526
45172CB00001B/245